HELLO

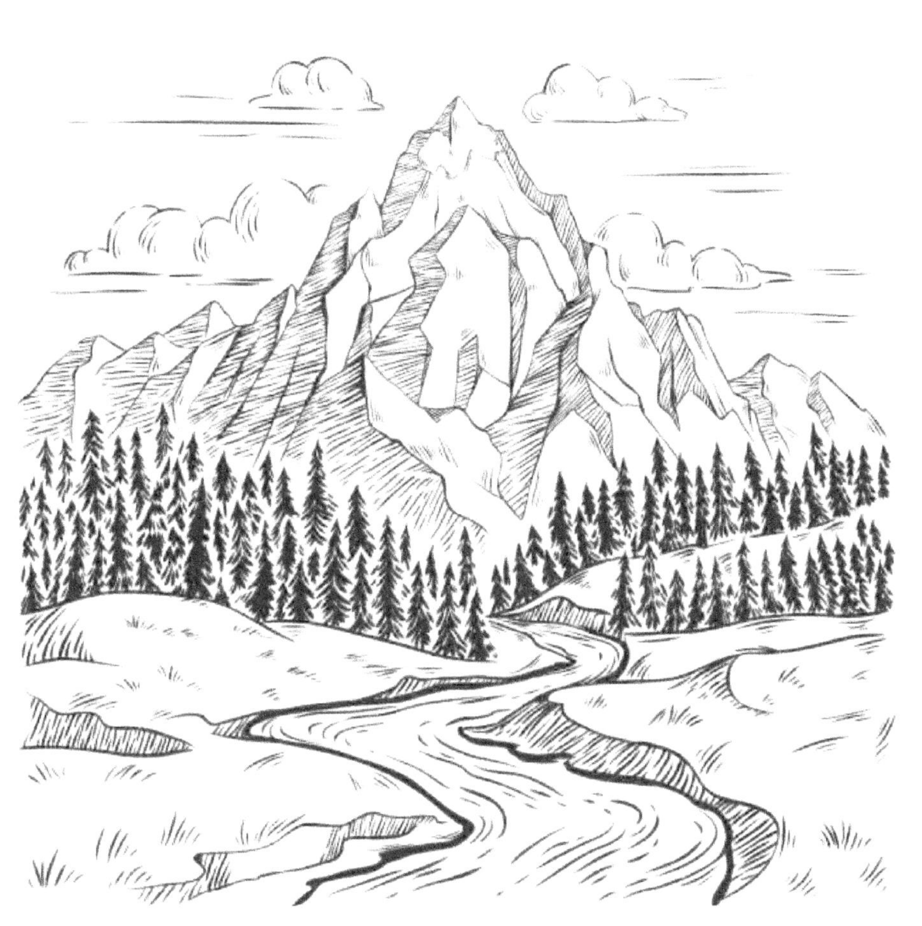

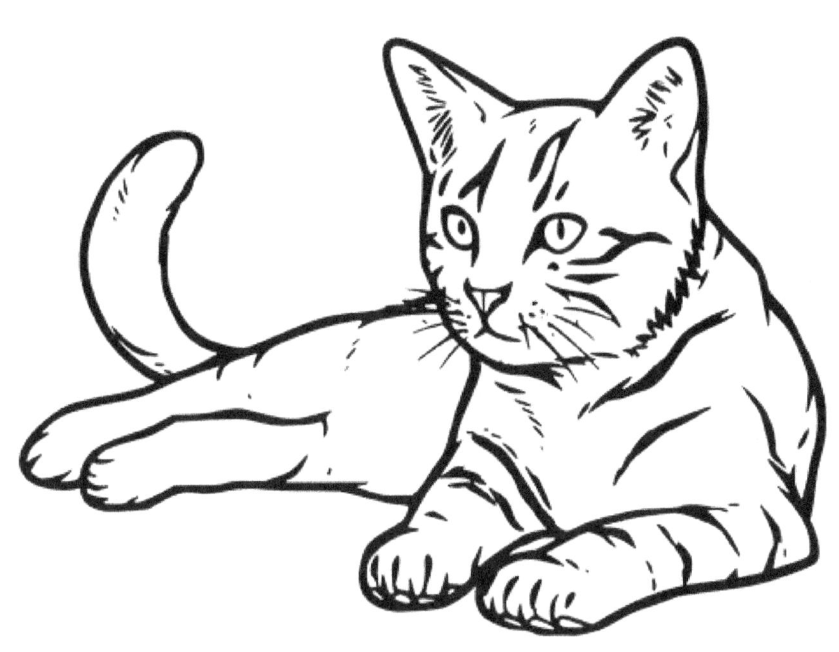

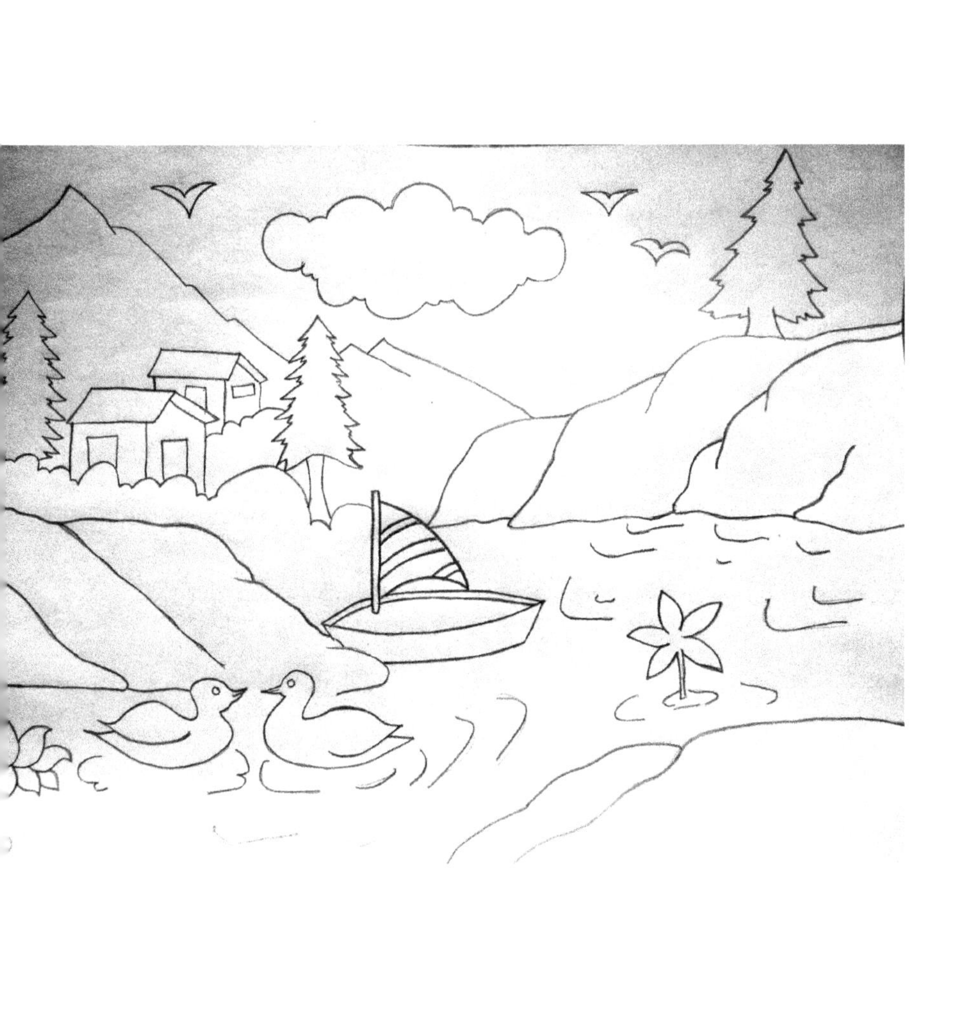

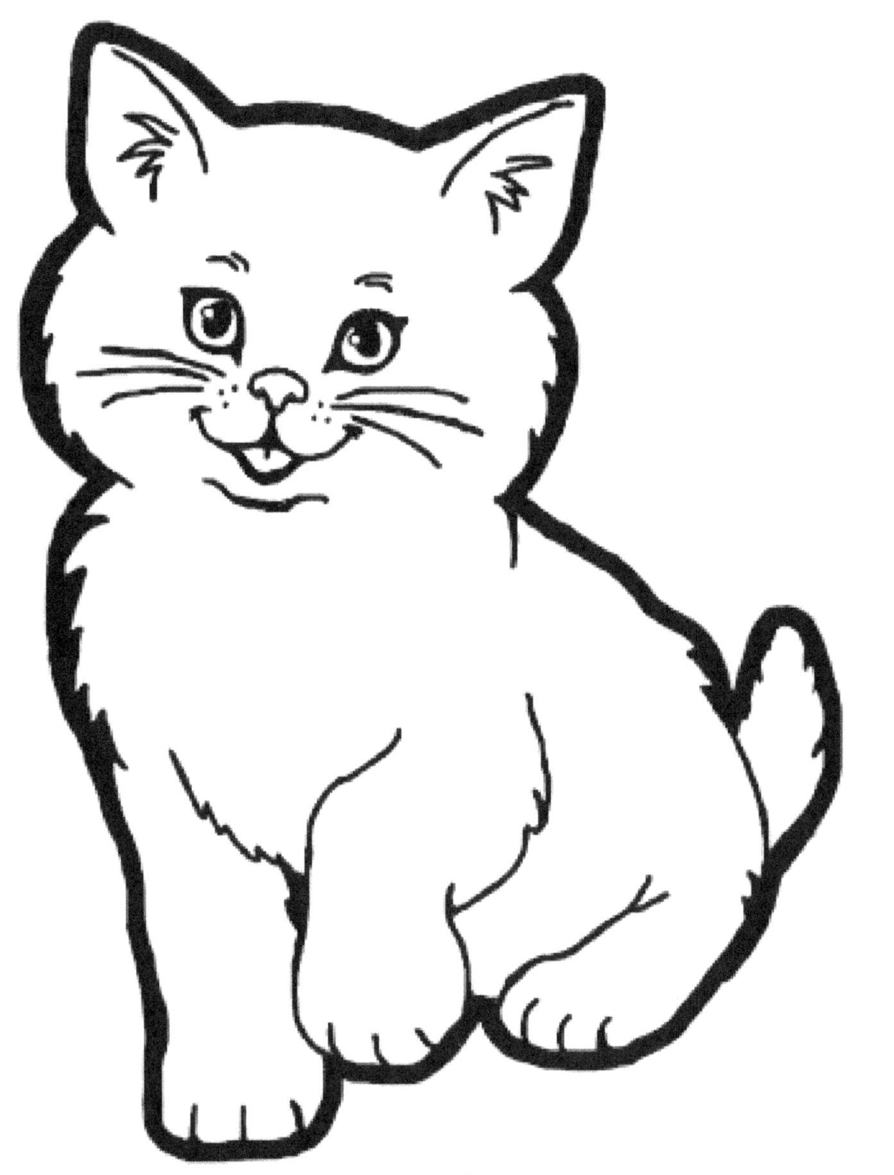

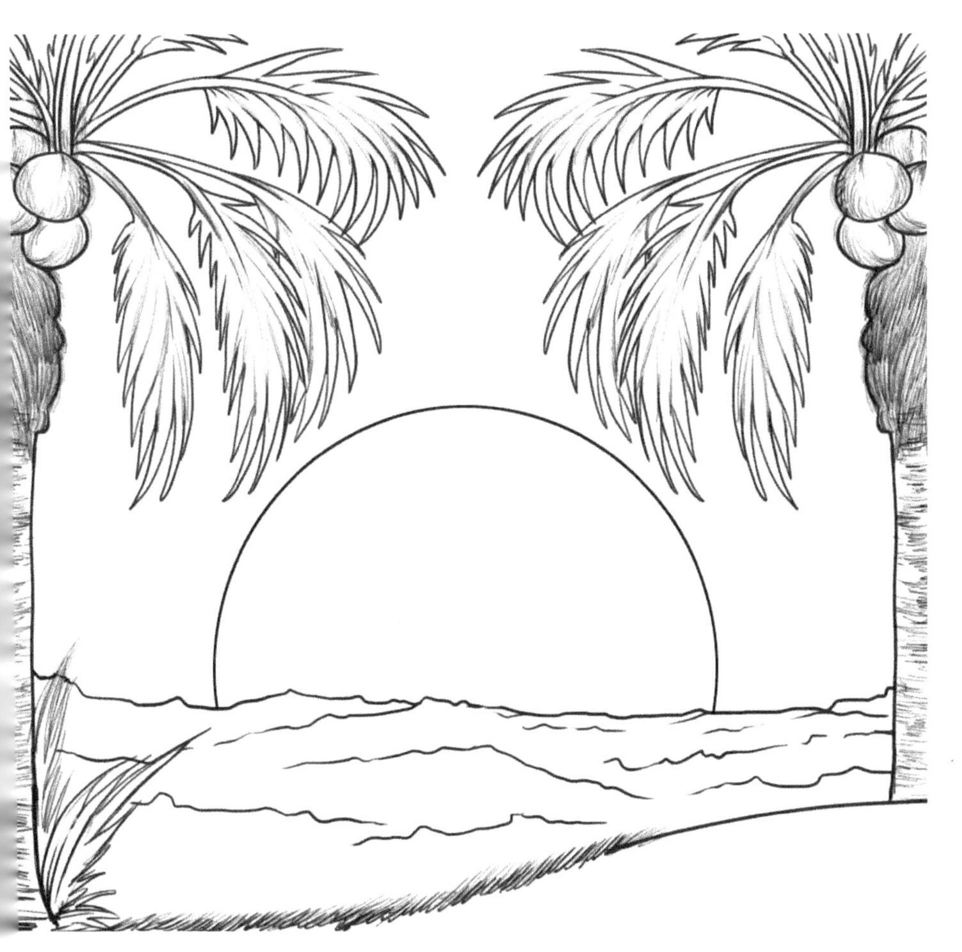

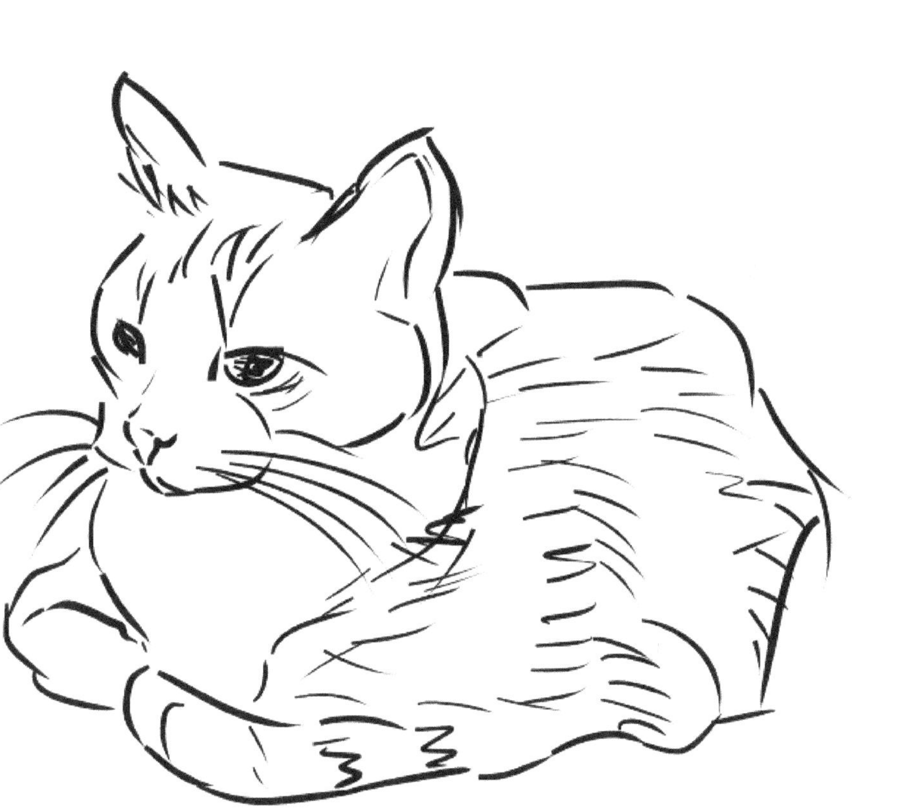

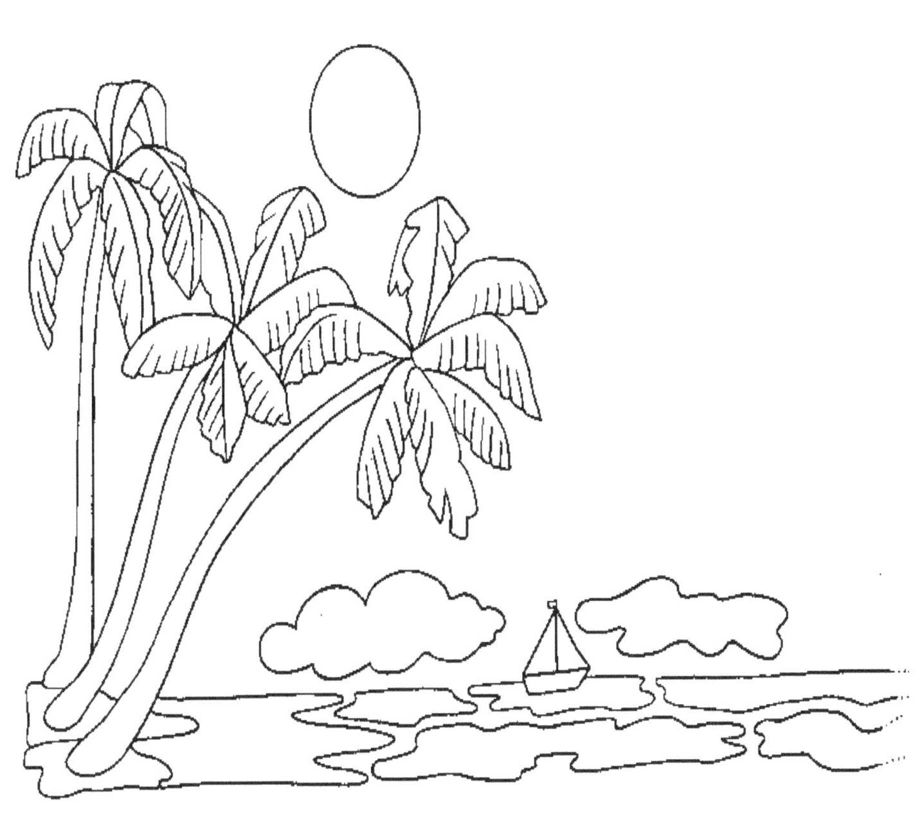

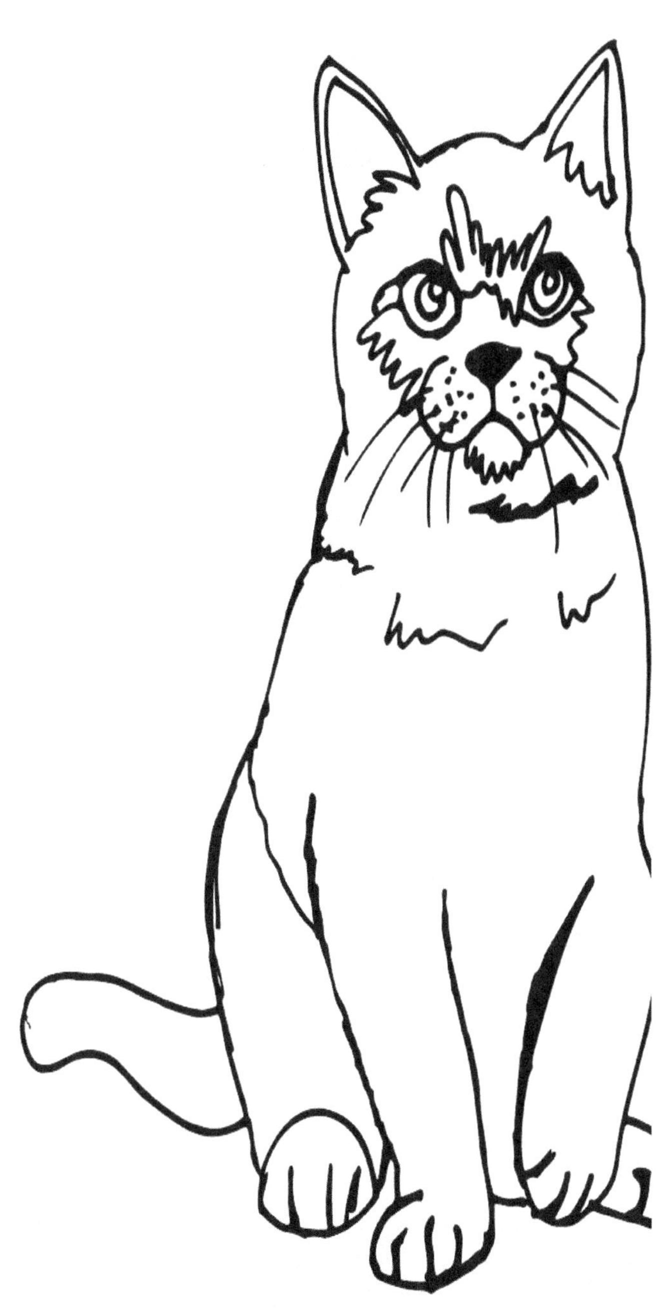

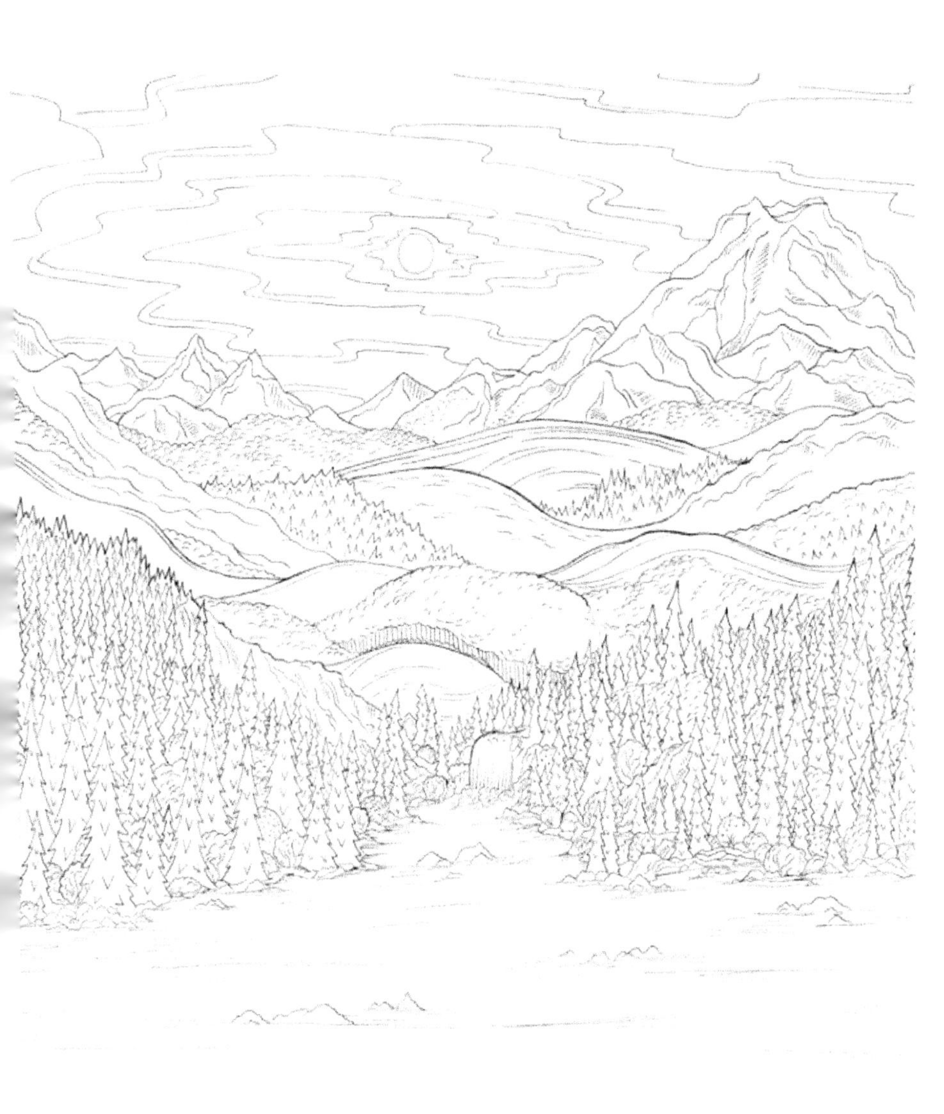

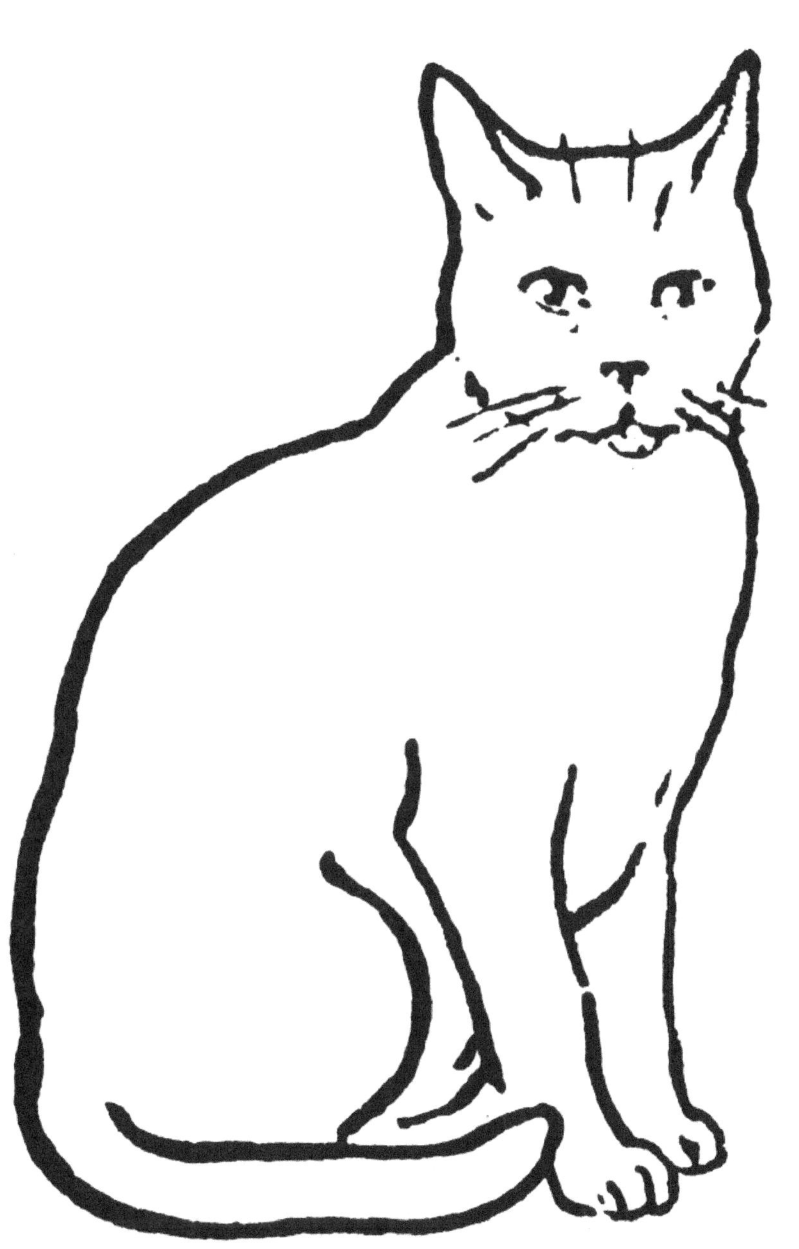

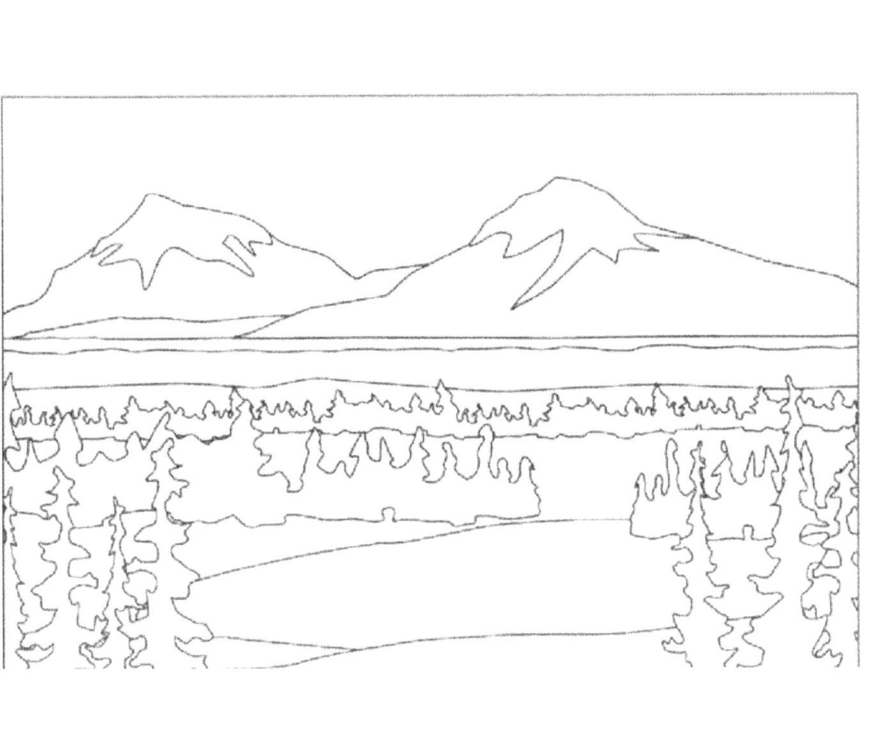

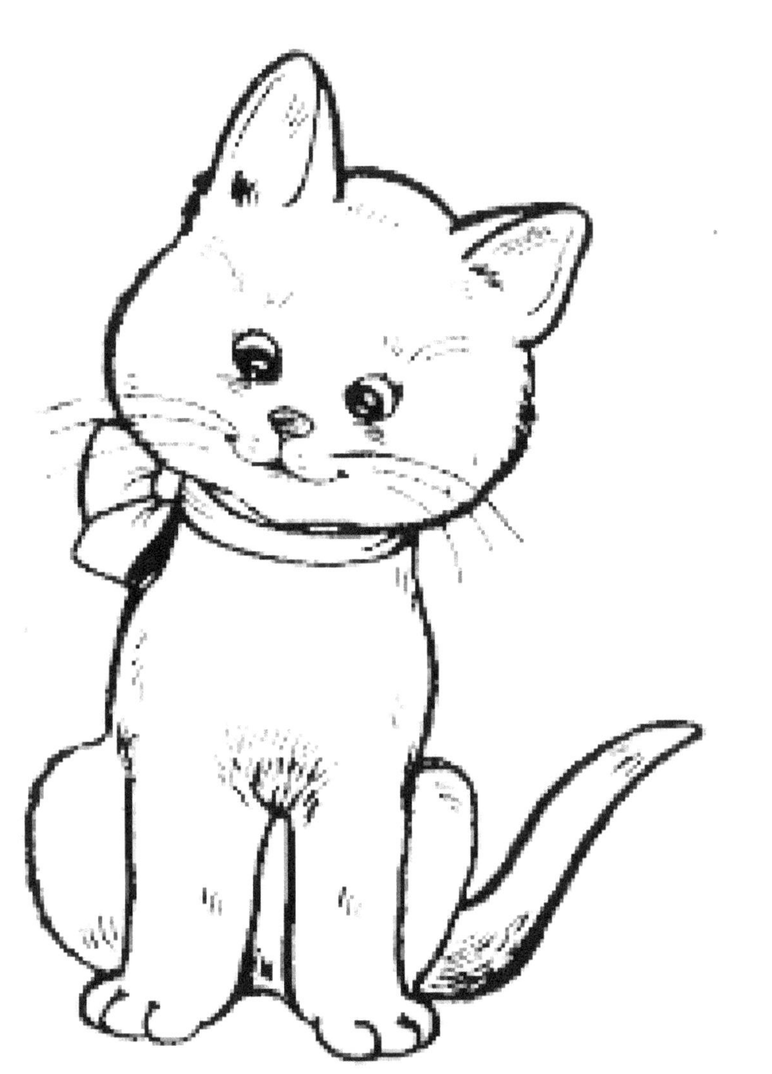

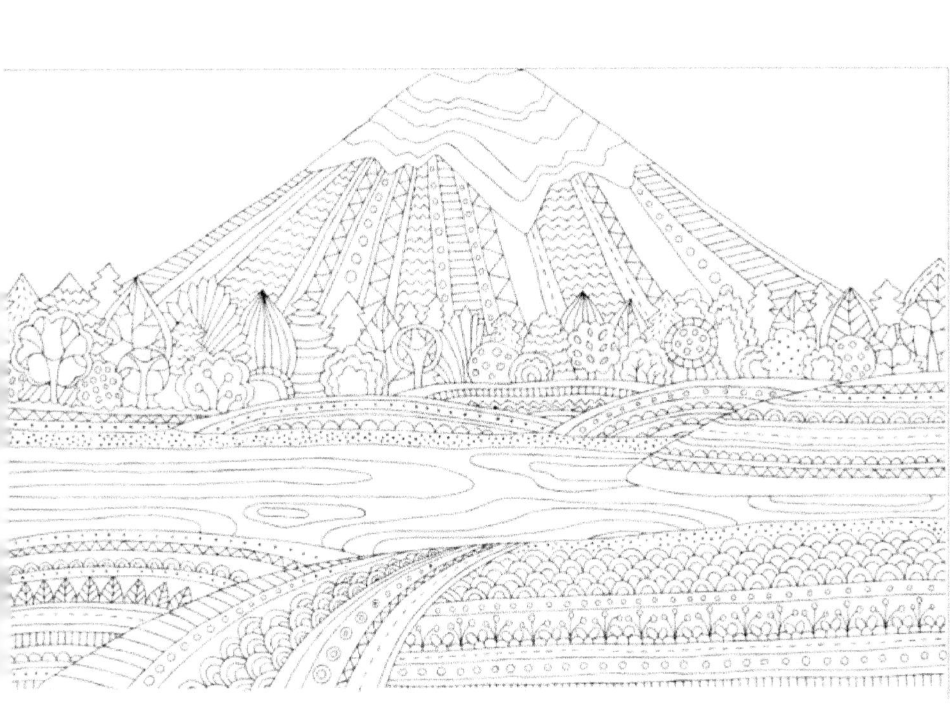

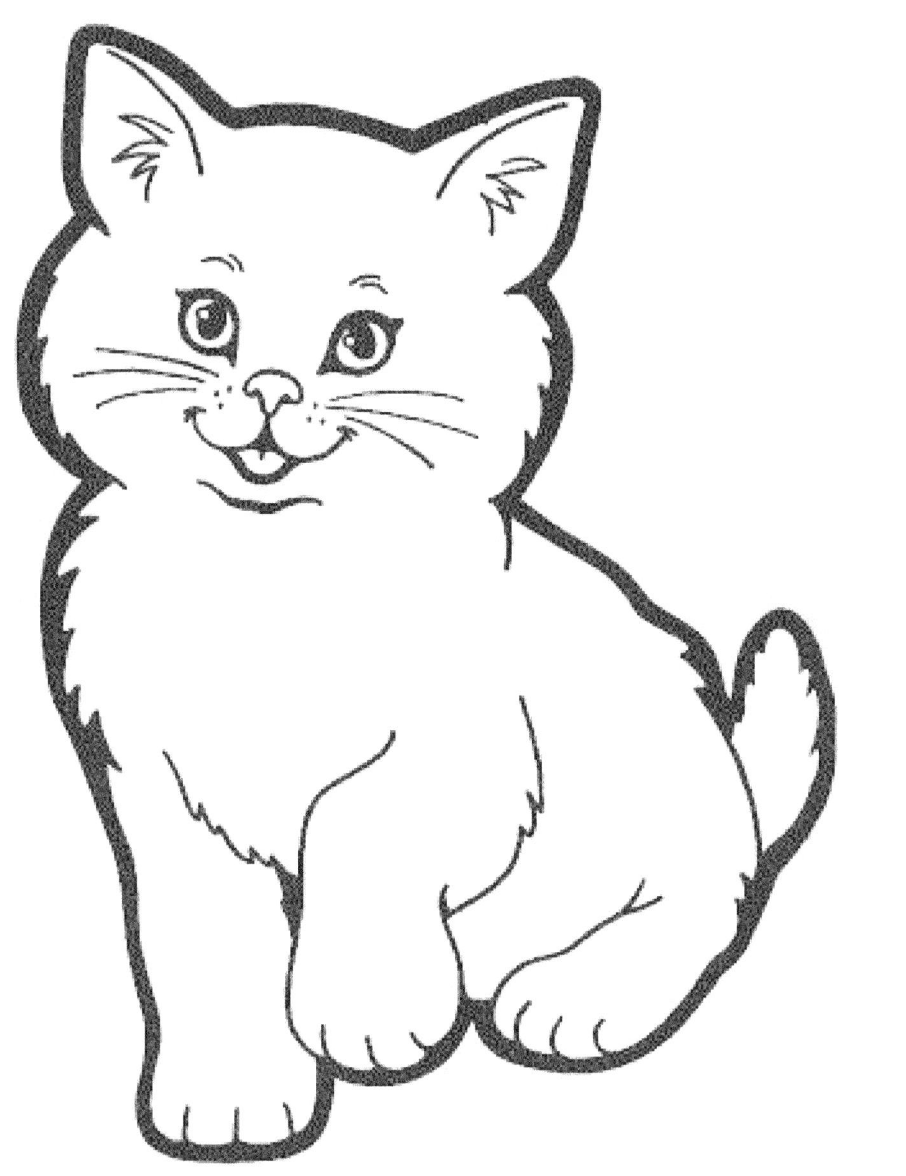

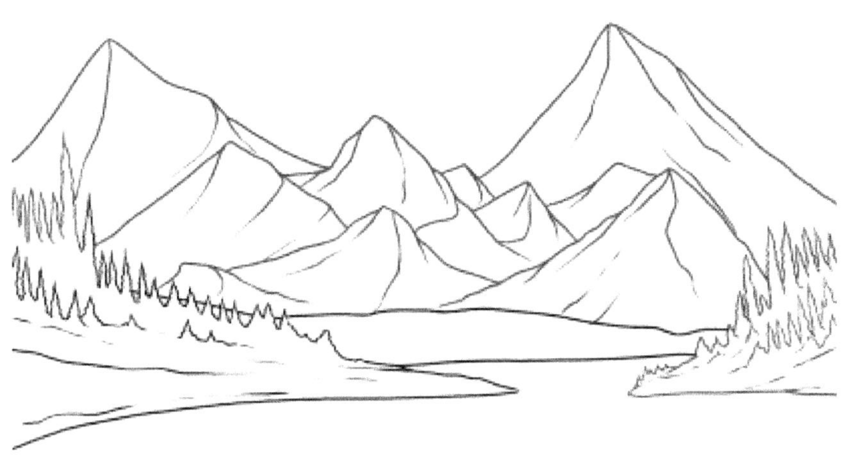

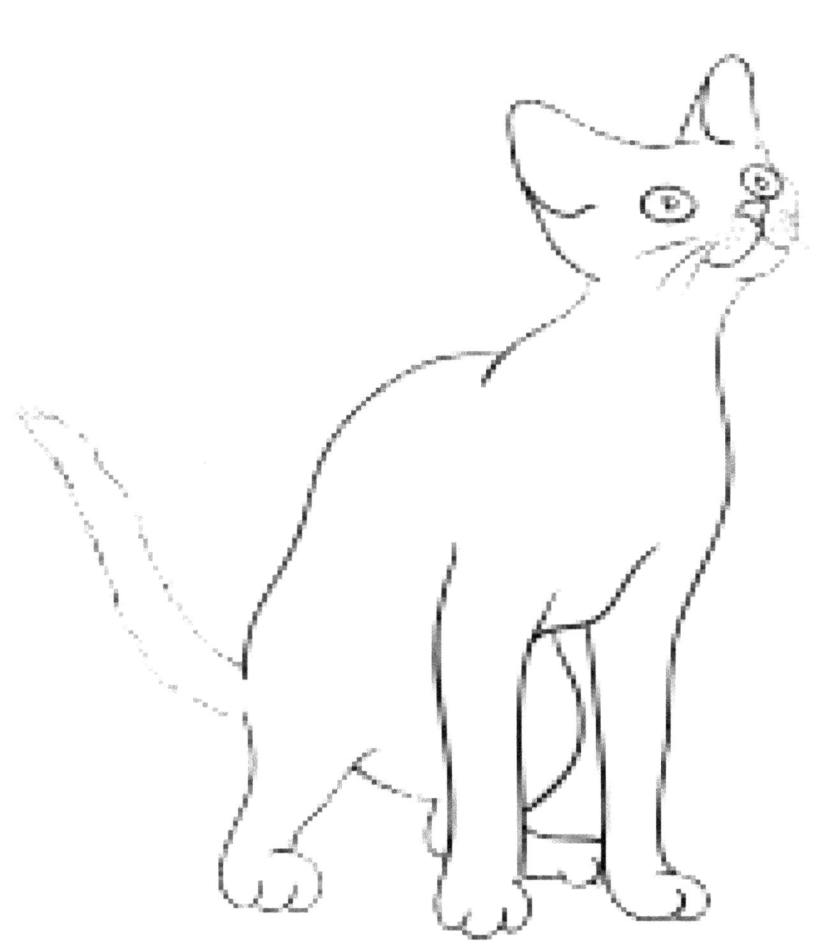

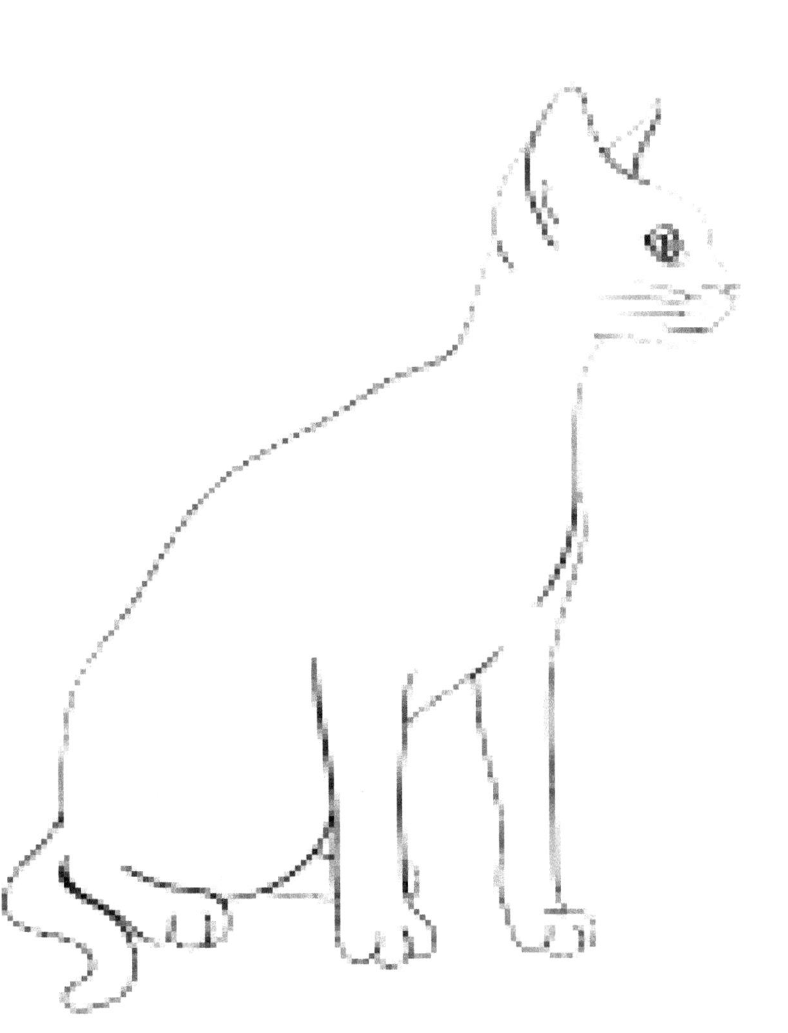

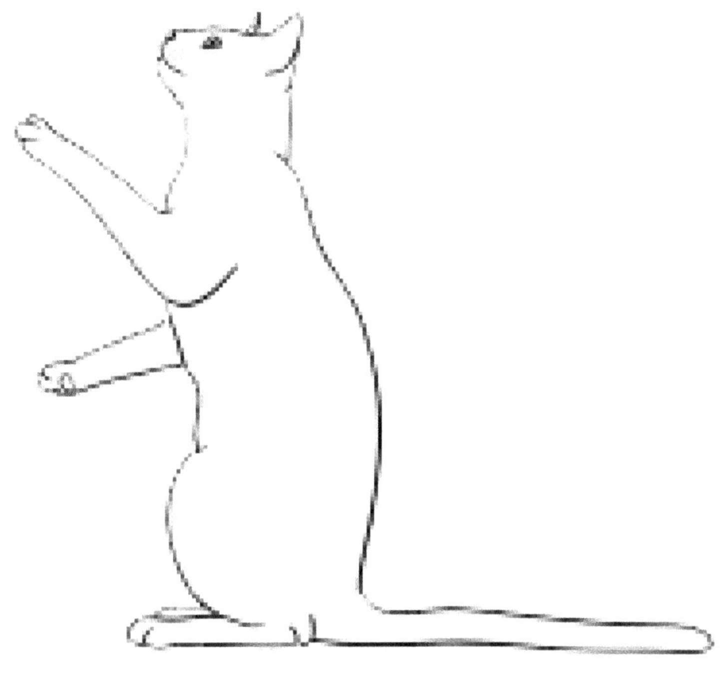

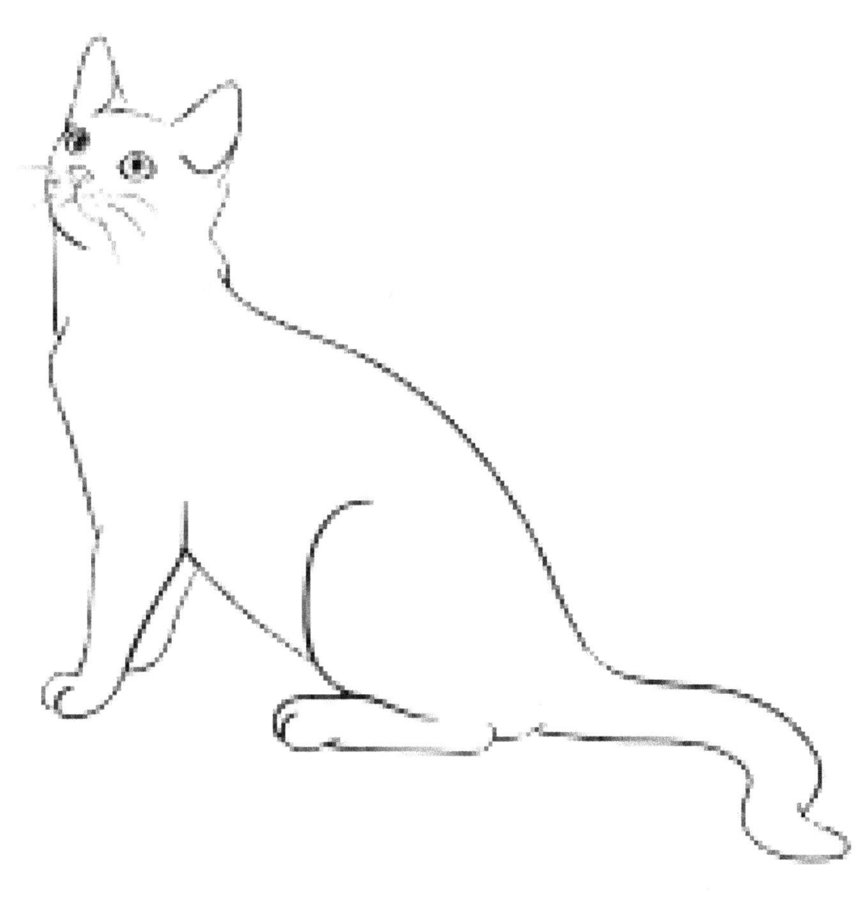

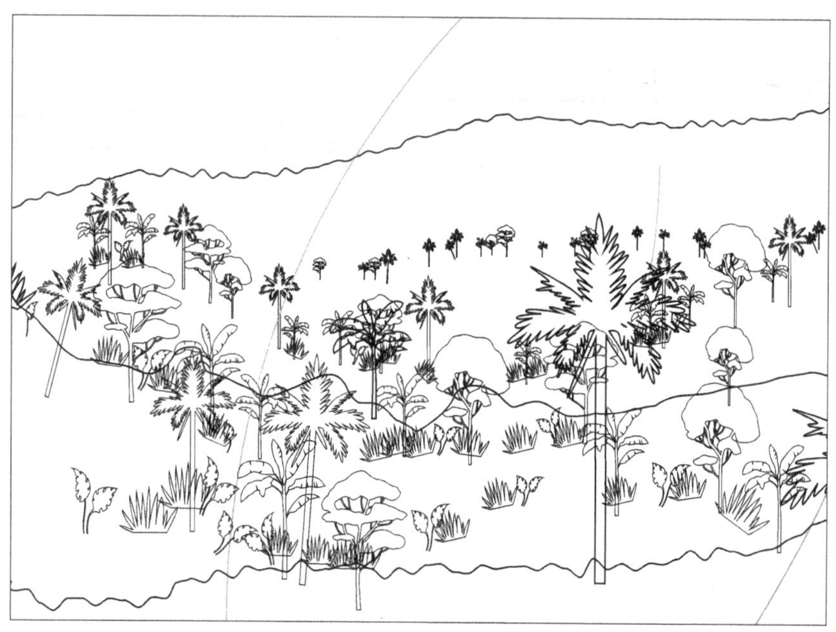

THIS COLORING BOOK BELONGS TO :

____